NATALIE IMBRUGLIA :
LEFT OF THE MIDDLE

EXCLUSIVE DISTRIBUTORS: MUSIC SALES LIMITED 8/9 FRITH STREET, LONDON W1V 5TZ, ENGLAND. > MUSIC SALES PTY LIMITED 120 ROTHSCHILD AVENUE, ROSEBERY, NSW 2018, AUSTRALIA. >
ORDER NO.AM952380 > ISBN 0-7119-7105-6 > THIS BOOK © COPYRIGHT 1997 BY WISE PUBLICATIONS. > VISIT THE INTERNET MUSIC SHOP AT http://www.musicsales.co.uk
UNAUTHORISED REPRODUCTION OF ANY PART OF THIS PUBLICATION BY ANY MEANS INCLUDING PHOTOCOPYING IS AN INFRINGEMENT OF COPYRIGHT. > MUSIC ARRANGED BY DEREK JONES. >
MUSIC PROCESSED BY PAUL EWERS MUSIC DESIGN. > PRINTED IN GREAT BRITAIN BY PRINTWISE (HAVERHILL) LIMITED, HAVERHILL, SUFFOLK. > YOUR GUARANTEE OF QUALITY:
AS PUBLISHERS, WE STRIVE TO PRODUCE EVERY BOOK TO THE HIGHEST COMMERCIAL STANDARDS. > THE MUSIC HAS BEEN FRESHLY ENGRAVED AND, WHILST ENDEAVOURING TO RETAIN
THE ORIGINAL RUNNING ORDER OF THE RECORDED ALBUM, THE BOOK HAS BEEN CAREFULLY DESIGNED TO MINIMISE AWKWARD PAGE TURNS AND TO MAKE PLAYING FROM IT A REAL PLEASURE. >
PARTICULAR CARE HAS BEEN GIVEN TO SPECIFYING ACID-FREE, NEUTRAL-SIZED PAPER MADE FROM PULPS WHICH HAVE NOT BEEN ELEMENTAL CHLORINE BLEACHED. > THIS PULP IS FROM
FARMED SUSTAINABLE FORESTS AND WAS PRODUCED WITH SPECIAL REGARD FOR THE ENVIRONMENT. > THROUGHOUT, THE PRINTING AND BINDING HAVE BEEN PLANNED TO ENSURE A STURDY,
ATTRACTIVE PUBLICATION WHICH SHOULD GIVE YEARS OF ENJOYMENT. > IF YOUR COPY FAILS TO MEET OUR HIGH STANDARDS, PLEASE INFORM US AND WE WILL GLADLY REPLACE IT. >
MUSIC SALES' COMPLETE CATALOGUE DESCRIBES THOUSANDS OF TITLES AND IS AVAILABLE IN FULL COLOUR SECTIONS BY SUBJECT, DIRECT FROM MUSIC SALES LIMITED. > PLEASE STATE YOUR
AREAS OF INTEREST AND SEND A CHEQUE/POSTAL ORDER FOR £1.50 FOR POSTAGE TO: MUSIC SALES LIMITED, NEWMARKET ROAD, BURY ST. EDMUNDS, SUFFOLK IP33 3YB. >>

WISE PUBLICATIONS
LONDON / NEW YORK / SYDNEY / PARIS / COPENHAGEN / MADRID

TORN

WORDS & MUSIC > ANNE PREVEN, SCOTT CUTLER & PHIL THORNALLEY

Lyrics:

I thought I saw— a man— brought to life,— he was warm, he came a-round— like he was dig-ni-fied,— he showed me what it was— to cry.

CHORUS

(See block lyric for final chorus)

Final chorus:
I'm all out of faith
This is how I feel
I'm cold and I'm ashamed
Bound and broken on the floor.
You're a little late
I'm already torn...
Torn...

BIG MISTAKE > >

WORDS & MUSIC > NATALIE IMBRUGLIA & MARK GOLDENBERG

1. There's no sign on the gate and there's mud on your face,
(Verses 2 & 3 see block lyric))

don't you think it's time we re-in-ves-ti-gate this sit-u-a-tion,

D.%. al Coda

Coda

(1, 3.) And you're down on your knees, it's too late. Oh
(2.) And you cry over me, I can't wait. I

don't come crawl - in'. And you lie by my feet, what a big mis - take.
feel you stall - in'. And you try to reach me, what a big mis - take.

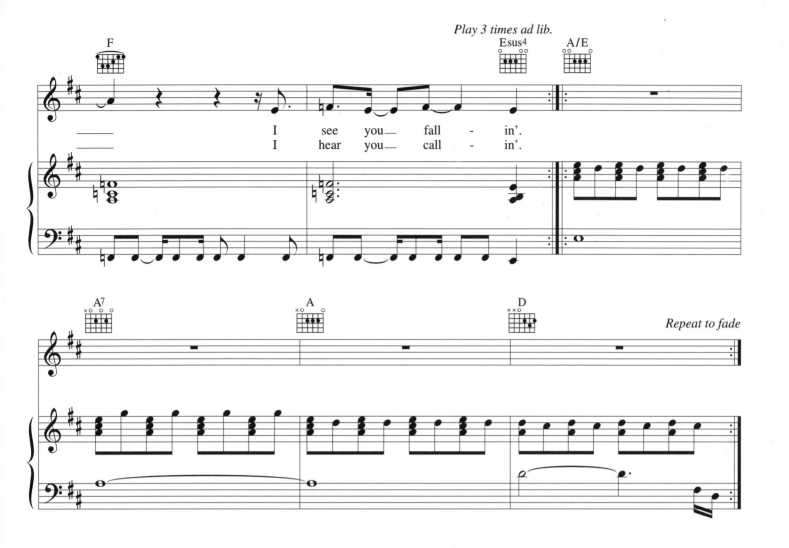

Verse 2:
Got a buzz in my head
And my flowers are dead
Can't figure out a way to rectify this situation
Don't believe what you said.

You forgotten how it started *etc.*

Verse 3:
I could sting like a bee
Careful how you treat me
Baby I don't think I'll accept your sorry invitation
Close the door as you leave.

You forgotten how it started *etc.*

LEAVE ME ALONE > >

WORDS & MUSIC > NATALIE IMBRUGLIA & ANDY WRIGHT

leave me a - lone,___ just leave me a - lone.___

Da de da de da de da de da.

Verse 2:
You like me to stroke you
Careful I don't choke you
Did you read my mind?
You say don't be blue
Is that the best you can do?
I've lost my patience now.

Oh leave me alone *etc.*

INTUITION

WORDS & MUSIC > NATALIE IMBRUGLIA, PHIL THORNALLEY & DAVE MUNDAY

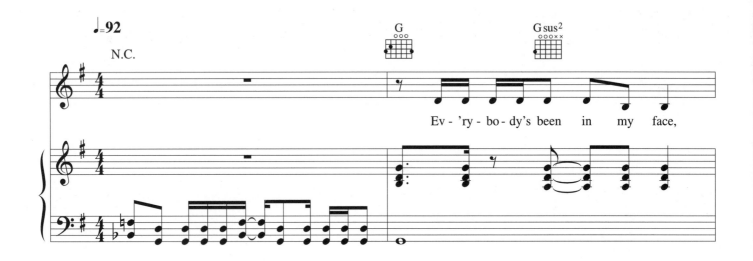

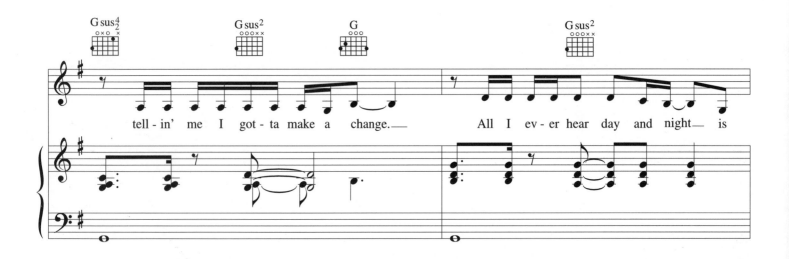

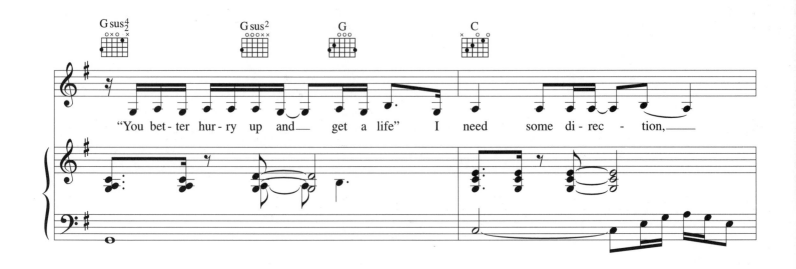

And all I can say is in-tu-
-i-tion tells me how to live my day. In-tu-i-tion tells me
when to walk a-way. Could have turned left, could have turned right, but I
end-ed up here bang— in the mid-dle of a re-al life.

Should have turned left but I turned right and I end-ed up here, and I feel al-

right.

You make it hard— for me.— Can't find the re - al you.—

You real - ly think that I___ can see___ what it is that you're try-

-right,   I feel al - right.   'Cause I feel al -

-right,   I feel al - right.   'Cause I feel al - right.

Verse 2:
Then another one always says
She'd do anything to get ahead
She doesn't care if she has to scratch
And claw to get in the door
She wants her fifteen minutes of fame
And twenty would be nice
But I guess it's her life.

'Cause intuition tells me that I'm doin' fine
Intuition tells me when to draw the line
Could have turned left, could have turned right
But I ended up here bang in the middle of a real life.

SMOKE > >

WORDS & MUSIC > NATALIE IMBRUGLIA & MATT BRONLEEWEE

Where are you dad? Mum's look-in' sad,

1.

what's up with that? It's dark— in here.

Why_____ bleed-ing is— breath-ing, you're hid-ing

un - der - neath— the smoke in the room._____ Try,_____

bleed-ing is__ be - liev - ing,   I   used to.

I   used__ to.__

Why_____ bleed-ing is__ breath - ing,   you're hid - ing

Verse 2:
My mouth is dry
Forgot how to cry
What's up with that?
You're hurting me
I'm running fast
Can't hide the past
What's up with that?

ONE MORE ADDICTION > >

WORDS & MUSIC > NATALIE IMBRUGLIA, PHIL THORNALLEY & DAVE MUNDAY

1. First the good___ news, it's gon-na feel ve-ry nice. Then the bad
(Verse 2 see block lyric)

___ news, you got-ta pay a hea-vy price. Rip tide, we slide, we ride on a

deep for-bid-den sea.___ Un-der we go so slow, and you're hang-ing on___ to me.___ And I___ say

Take a breath, let it out. All the things you frown a-bout are mean-ing-less of course, un - less you're do-ing this for real. I guess I meant to but I don't know what is in the way and could I say it's you I bet I won't for- get. May-be I'm not rea - dy yet. Oh, oh

Verse 2:
I reject you, but I can't follow through
I'd forget you, but you'd end up tappin' on my back door
Somehow I lost myself in a tunnel long and black
Somewhere at the end, I pretend, there's a way of turning back.

And I say oh, oh one more addiction *etc.*

WORDS & MUSIC > NATALIE IMBRUGLIA & MARK GOLDENBERG

1. Got - ta get___ back,___ got - ta fig - ure out___ a way___
(Verse 2 see block lyric)

Tacet 1° -

Verse 2:

All alone but I'm in a crowded room
I'm sinking in quicksand tonight
You pick me up and I shine across the sky
Till morning, then you colour me in.
Guess it won't amount to much
Seems to me I've lost my touch
I'm back in line
Don't believe a thing they say today
Turn around and walk away
Everything will go your way, I pray
Seems we all get lost amongst the pigeons and the crumbs.

DON'T YOU THINK? > >

WORDS & MUSIC > PHIL THORNALLEY & COLIN CAMPSIE

Yeah some peo-ple   don't

wor-ry   a-bout no-thing,   don't know what's go-ing on.   I'm

Don't you think,— don't you think, don't you think— that may - be it's

time,_____ yes it's

time,_____

1.

it's time you start - ed think - ing.

It's time you start - ed think - ing.

It's time you start - ed think - ing.   It's time you start - ed think-

-ing.   Don't just   sweet - en up— the taste.   It's time you start - ed

2.

N.C.

think-ing 'bout things in the back of your head,   some-one said— be-fore you turn a blind eye.

Hear a bell ring, sex sells ev-'ry-thing but I don't buy— it, so don't try— it.

Sleep-ing in the small world, head in the sand, bet-ter wash your hands,— make a new plan.

There's more im-por-tant things than mak-ing sure your shoes walk just right.

Ig-nore re-a-li-ty.— There's no-thing you can do a-bout it.

Verse 2:
Brother shoots brother
But meanwhile you're fixing up your face
You're not affected by the truth unless it's on your doorstep
Deodorise your paradise, no point in getting crazy.

Don't you think *etc.*

WORDS & MUSIC > NATALIE IMBRUGLIA, RICK PALOMBI & NICK TREVISIK

1. Sweet con - fet - ti out look - ing for a sav - - - iour,
(Verse 2 see block lyric)

find - ing it hard to break the chain, noth - ing ven -

Tacet 1°

-tured noth-ing gained.— Ice-cream beau-ty, act-ing

on her best— be-hav - iour, find-ing it hard— to bite her tongue,—

— feel-ing so old— as the night is young.————

Six foot lean-ing on a li - zard chest,— two red dra-gons ir - oned

on his vest,— all that mo - ney you de - serve the best.— I'm im - pressed,—

F#dim   Fmaj7   Esus4   **1.** Am

— I'm im - pressed,— I'm im - pressed.—

F6   Am   F6   **2.**

N.C.

Ev - 'ry day— is like— your birth - day,

Verse 2:
What you've got isn't all that you've been given
Changing your body like you change your jeans
Nothing is ever as it seems
Something tells me it's a marriage made in heaven
Stealing your look from a magazine
Playing the part from a movie scene.

Six foot leaning *etc.*

WISHING I WAS THERE > >

WORDS & MUSIC > NATALIE IMBRUGLIA, PHIL THORNALLEY & COLIN CAMPSIE

1. Take your hand and place it in— my pock-et, flick your eyes back in— their sock-ets.—
(Verse 2 see block lyric)

think that's fair. Boy I'm not so dumb. But when you leave__

__ me__ I'll be wish-ing I,__ wish-ing I,__

wish-ing I__ was there.__

1.

I

2.

wish-ing I,__ wish-ing I,__ wish-ing I__ was there.__

1.

Wish-ing I,___ wish-ing I,___ wish-ing I___ was there___ with you.___

2.

wish-ing I___ was there___ with you.___ No don't say you love___

___ me,___ don't say you need___ me.___ I real - ly don't

think that's fair. Oh I'm not so dumb, but when you leave___ me___ I'll be

Verse 2:
I dreamt about another girl in bed with you
You just laughed and smiled, denied the proof
We're fine till I think of a problem
I wish it made sense, like a joke that no one gets
It's a life without regret
I want it to feel that way for ever and ever.

I know I get cold *etc.*

CITY > >

WORDS & MUSIC > NATALIE IMBRUGLIA & PHIL THORNALLEY

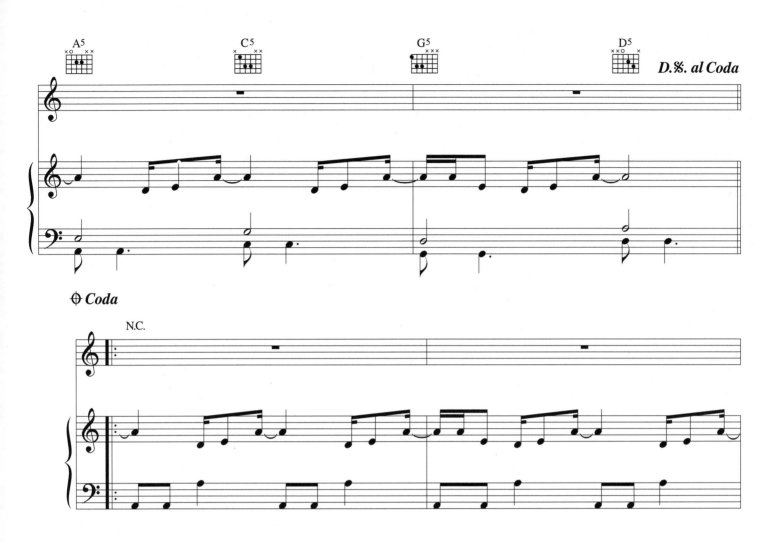

D.%. al Coda

⊕ *Coda*

Repeat ad lib. to fade

Verse 2:
Funny how those friends forget you
When you tire of their games
You miss a show or a party that blows
And they've forgotten your name, yeah
And you wonder what you've become
They pull you back when you try to run.

Well anybody heading in my direction *etc.*

Verse 3:
I left the me I used to be
I wanna see this through
I left the me I used to be
If only you'd see it too
Well I wonder what you've become
You pull me back when I try to run.

Well anybody heading in my direction *etc.*

LEFT OF THE MIDDLE > >

WORDS & MUSIC > NATALIE IMBRUGLIA & STEVE BOOKER

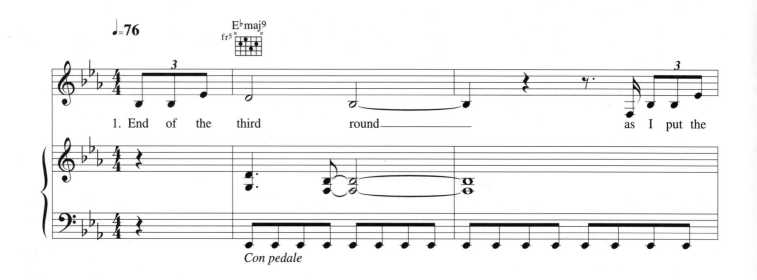

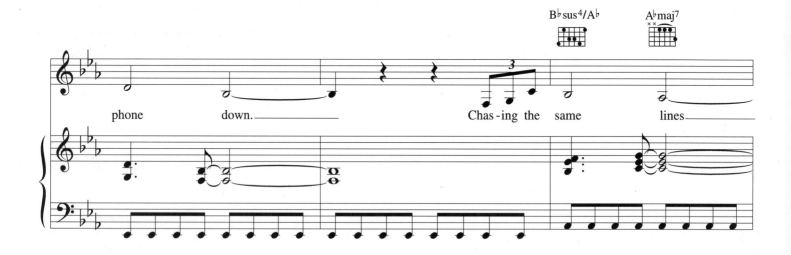

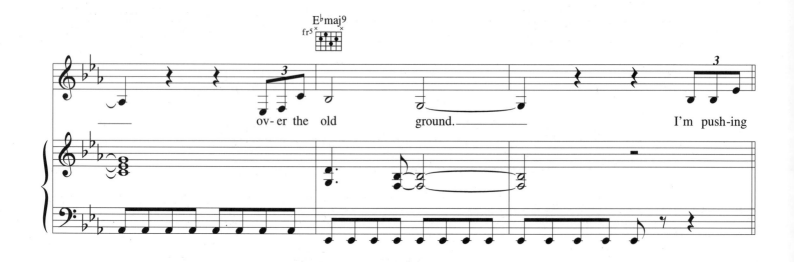

ze - - - ro,_____ where is my he - - ro._____
(Verse 2 see block lyric)

He's out there some - where_____ left of the

mid - dle._____ And your world___ falls_____ down.

And you're there___ call - ing out.___ But it's some-

- thing I_____ can't say, though it seems_____ the on - ly way.

But it's a game_____ that I_____ can't play,_____ not to - day.

2. I got my

And my world

Verse 2:

I got my ticket and I got a straight road
But I'm passing the same signs over and over.
And my world falls down
And I'm there calling out
But it's something I can't say *etc.*

2/99 (33397)